Engraved by A.L.Dick.

BRIAIN BOIROIMHE,

Monarch of Ireland. Anno. Dom. 1027.

New York. D & J. Sadlier.

THE HISTORY OF IRELAND

ANCIENT AND MODERN

Translated from the French of

THE ABBÈ MAC GEOGHEGAN

BY PATRICK O'KELLY, ESQ[R]

Approach to Cashel.
(from the North)

New York, D. & J. Sadlier.

THE HISTORY OF IRELAND,

ANCIENT AND MODERN,

TAKEN FROM THE MOST AUTHENTIC RECORDS,

AND

DEDICATED TO THE IRISH BRIGADE.

BY THE ABBÉ MAC-GEOGHEGAN

TRANSLATED FROM THE FRENCH,

BY PATRICK O'KELLY, ESQ.,

Author of a History of the Irish Rebellion of 1798, &c.

"Let Erin remember the days of old,
Ere her faithless sons betray'd her:
When Malachi wore the collar of gold,
Which he won from the proud invader;
When her kings, with standard of green unfurl'd,
Led the Red-Branch Knights to danger;
Ere the emerald gem of the western world
Was set in the crown of a stranger."

MOORE.

NEW YORK:

D. & J. SADLIER, 58 GOLD-STREET.

PREFACE

One of the most important works that have ever been written respecting Ireland, is the history of the Abbé Mac-Geoghegan. It may be a matter of surprise to the unthinking, that this most valuable and interesting history has not before this been translated into English; but this surprise must be lessened when we reflect, that, besides the distracted situation of this country, and the passions that have agitated her different sects and parties, there were other more powerful causes which might have prevented the publication of the great truths contained in this rare history of Ireland.

Under such circumstances it cannot be wondered at, that an impartial history, which has made known to France and to the Continent the wrongs and the sufferings of Ireland, and one that has accurately displayed the conduct of her enemies, and the struggles of her friends, should, even to this period, be unknown to the English reader.

The elegantly written calumnies of Hume have been generally circulated, while the plain truths of Mac-Geoghegan have been suppressed.

The circumstances which have given an impetus to the circulation of fiction, and the discountenancing of fact, are now at an end. The bad passions of Irishmen are subsiding, and the settlement of a great question (Catholic Emancipation) has taken away from all parties an interest in the concealment of what was just, while it has given to the people of all classes an inducement to know the truth alone, and nothing but the truth. With these objects solely, the translation of the work of the Abbé Mac-Geoghegan has been undertaken.

The history of Ireland is generally complained of even in Ireland, while the ignorance of it in England has entailed upon Irishmen great and innumerable calamities. It is only by a knowledge of our country, that Englishmen can know how to estimate its worth, and, until a full and accurate knowledge of all its circumstances are attained, can the country expect justice to be done to it. Those, therefore, should be deemed the best friends to Ireland, who exert themselves to induce their fellow-men to study her character, to know her situation, and to appreciate her value.

With such objects has the author of this Translation undertaken the risk of giving to both countries the work of the Abbé Mac-Geoghegan; and from Irishmen at least, he looks with confidence for that support and patronage which patriotism alone should induce them to afford him.

He begs the liberty, therefore, of subscribing himself their very humble and devoted servant,

PATRICK O'KELLY.

N. B. *Some portions of this valuable history were unavoidably omitted in the former edition, translated by Mr. O'Kelly, but they shall be inserted in this edition, which has been carefully revised and corrected by the Translator.*

DEDICATION

TO THE IRISH TROOPS IN THE SERVICE OF FRANCE.

GENTLEMEN,

To you I owe the homage of my labor; you owe to it the honor of your protection. The history of Ireland belongs to you, as being that of your ancestors; it is their shades that I invoke in a foreign land; it is their glory that I recall. The records of their exploits and virtues, which fill a space of so many ages, I here bring to your review.

Among all the virtues, whereof you shall see so many brilliant examples, you will remark two that were peculiarly dear to your ancestors, viz., an ardent zeal for the true religion so soon as they were made acquainted with it, and an inviolable fidelity to their kings: such are the qualities, gentlemen, which still characterize you.

Europe, towards the end of the last century, was surprised to see your fathers abandon the delights of a fertile country, renounce the advantages which an illustrious birth had given them in their native land, and tear themselves from their possessions, from kindred, friends, and from all that nature and fortune had made dear to them; she was astonished to behold them deaf to the proposals of a liberal usurper, and following the fortunes of a fugitive king, to seek with him, in foreign climes, fatigues and danger, content with their misfortune, as the seal of their fidelity to unhappy masters.

France, which among so many virtues (of which she is a model) places in the first rank loyalty to her kings, was delighted to see those strangers dispute with her the glory of it: she gladly opened to them a generous bosom, being persuaded that men so devoted to their princes, would not be less so to their benefactors; and felt a pleasure in seeing them march under her banners. Your ancestors have not disappointed her hopes. Nervinde, Marseilles, Barcelona, Cremona, Luzara,

Spire, Castiglione, Almanza, Villa Viciosa,* and many other places, witnesses of their immortal valor, consecrated their devotedness for the new country which had adopted them. France applauded their zeal, and the greatest of monarchs raised their praise to the highest pitch by honoring them with the flattering title of "his brave Irishmen."

The example of their chiefs animated their courage; the Viscounts Mountcashel† and Clare,‡ the Count of Lucan,§ the Dillons, Lees, Rothes, O'Donnels, Fitzgeralds, Nugents, and Galmoys,‖ opened to them on the borders of the Meuse, the Rhine, and the Po, the career of glory, while the O'Mahonys, MacDonnels, Lawlesses, the Lacys, the Burks, O'Carrols, Craftons, Comerford, Gardner, and O'Connor, crowned themselves with laurels on the shores of the Tagus.

The neighboring powers wished to have in their service the children of those great men; Spain retained some of you near her throne. Naples invited you to her fertile country: Germany called you to the defence of her eagles. The Taffs, the Hamiltons, O'Dwyers,¶ Browns, Wallaces, and O'Neills, supported the majesty of the empire, and were intrusted with its most important posts. The ashes of Mareschal Brown,** are every day watered with the tears of the soldiers to whom he was so dear, while the O'Donnels, Maguires, Lacys, and others, endeavored to form themselves after the example of that great man.

Russia, that vast and powerful empire, an empire which has passed suddenly from obscurity to so much glory, wished to learn the military discipline from your corps. Peter the Great, that penetrating genius and hero, the creator of a nation which is now triumphant, thought he could not do better than confide that essential part of the art of war to the Field Mareschal de Lacy; and the worthy daughter of that great emperor, always intrusted to that warrior the principal defence of the august throne which she filled with so much glory. Finally the Viscount Fermoy,†† general officer in the service of Sardinia, has merited all the confidence of that crown.

But why recall those times that are so long past? Why do I seek your heroes in those distant regions? Permit me, Gentlemen, to bring to your recollection that great day, for ever memorable in the annals of France; let me remind you of the plains of Fontenoy, so precious to your glory; those plains were in con-

* M. de Vendôme, called the Chevalier de Bellerive, who had a particular esteem for that warlike nation, at the head of whose sons he had fought so many battles and gained so many victories, confessed that he was surprised at the dreadful feats that these army-butchers (as he called them) had performed in his presence.—*Camp de Vendome*, p. 224.

† M'Carthy. ‡ O'Brien. § Sarsfield. ‖ Butler.

¶ General O'Dwyer was commander of Belgrade.

** He was nephew of General Brown.

†† Roche, otherwise de la Roche.

cert with chosen French troops, the valiant Count of Thomond* being at your head, you charged with so much valor an enemy so formidable; animated by the presence of the august sovereign who rules over you, you contributed with so much success, to the gaining of a victory, which, till then, appeared doubtful. Lawfeld beheld you, two years afterwards, in concert with one of the most illustrious corps of France,† force intrenchments which appeared to be impregnable. Menin, Ypres, Tournay, saw you crown yourselves with glory under their walls, while your countrymen, under the standards of Spain, performed prodigies of valor at Campo Sancto and at Veletri.

But while I am addressing you, a part of your corps is flying to the defence of the allies of Louis,‡ another is sailing over the seas to seek amidst the waves another hemisphere, the eternal enemies of his empire.§

Behold, gentlemen, what all Europe contemplates in you; behold herein the qualities which have gained esteem for you, even from your most unjust enemies. Could a compatriot to whom the glory of Ireland is so dear, refuse to you his admiration? Accept, gentlemen, this small tribute of it.

Honor with your support a history, which the love for my country has caused me to undertake; your protection and patronage will render this work respectable, and may merit some indulgence for its defects; it should have none, were my labor and zeal equal to render it worthy of those to whom I dedicate it.

I am, with profound respect,

Gentlemen,

Your very humble and most obedient servant,

J. MAC-GEOGHEGAN.

* At present Mareschal of France, Knight of the Order of the Holy Ghost, Commander of Languedoc.

† The King's Regiment.

‡ The regiment of Fitzjames, composed of Irish cavalry, in the army of the Prince of Suabia, distinguished itself at the battle of Rosbach, against the Prussians.

§ General Lally, with his regiment, embarked for Pondicherry.

INTRODUCTION

To observe order and system in writing this history, I have thought proper to divide it into three parts, the objects of which appeared to me equally interesting. The first comprises the times which had passed from the establishment of the Scoto-Milesians in Ireland, down to the first century; that part, therefore, during which the island had been buried in the darkness of paganism, I call "Pagan Ireland."

The second commences with the beginning of Christianity in that country in the fifth, and continues until the twelfth century: this part I call "Christian Ireland."

Lastly, the third comprises the different invasions of the English, their establishment in that country, and all that has occurred down to our time.

In the first part, or Pagan Ireland, will be seen, first, the natural history of the country; second, a critical essay on the antiquities of the Milesians; third, the fabulous history of the Gadelians; fourth, the religion and customs of the Milesians; fifth, their civil and political government; sixth, their domestic and foreign wars; seventh, the different names under which that country has been known to the natives and to strangers; eighth, its general and particular divisions, its dynasties, and territories; also, the names and origin of those who were the proprietors of it.

In the second part, or Christian Ireland, will be seen, besides its profane history, the great progress that religion and learning had made from the fifth to the ninth century; the confusion caused to the state, and the disorder which prevailed in the church for some time, by the invasion of the Danes; tranquillity restored, and the exercise of religion re-established in its ancient splendor after the final defeat of those barbarians, which happened in the beginning of the eleventh century, until the arrival of the English towards the end of the twelfth.

Lastly, in the third part shall be described the manner in which some English colonies came to establish themselves in Ireland in the twelfth century; the wars which they made upon the old inhabitants of the country during four hundred years; the reunion of the two people in the reign of James VI. of Scotland and I. of England; finally, we shall conclude by giving a detail of the strange revolutions which have, since that time, arisen to Ireland.

BIOGRAPHICAL SKETCH

OF

THE AUTHOR.

The times in which the writer of this work was born, form so remarkable an epoch in the History of Ireland, that, before I enter into any account of his early life, it may not be amiss to make some remarks upon the principal features by which they were characterized. Ireland was then, in very truth, suffering, prostrate, trodden to the earth, and ground down by every kind of oppression, the most iniquitous and tyrannical. Every vestige of freedom was obliterated, and the remnants of her ancient glory still visible, bearing the marks of recent violence, spoke but too eloquently of the past, while they seemed but little calculated to awaken hopes of future amelioration. Every thing bore an aspect drear and desolate; whole towns and villages were forsaken. Here stood the dilapidated tower; there the ruined abbey, its altar desecrated and its shrines polluted; while its inmates, hunted like the game of the hills, endeavored

> —— "in a strange land to find
> That rest, which at home they had sought for in vain."

The war that placed William firmly on the English throne, and banished his imbecile and wretched predecessor, the unfortunate James, from the realm of his fathers, had been brought to a close before the walls of Limerick—"City of the violated treaty." The illustrious leader of Ireland's armies, Patrick Sarsfield, created "Earl of Lucan," and the other commanders, made their last stand within the walls of this city, where the articles of treaty were entered into, and in a short time after so basely violated, although ratified and sanctioned by the solemnity of an oath. And thus the "Island of the Betrayed," foolishly confiding in the honor of a monarch of England, having, besides, the apparently good security of his solemn oath, fell, the victim of perfidy, perjury, and broken faith, into the ruthless hands of the worst and the wickedest of tyrants. Every species of persecution was had recourse to against the professors of the Catholic faith, and every inducement held out to allure the people from the religion of their fathers. To prevent the education of future ministers, and deprive the people of a priesthood—the only safeguard of a faith, and the true source for its conveyance from generation to generation—all the iniquitous laws of Elizabeth were strictly enforced against the ecclesiastical institutions for the diffusion of theological and philosophical information. In a word, the bloody tragedies of Henry and his virgin daughter's reigns were reacted, with every addition which the improved taste, sharpened by the experience of the actors, could suggest.

The dreadful manner in which the Catholic clergy and people were treated, elicited the sympathy and commiseration of the rest of Europe. Among the many letters of condolence addressed to the clergy and people of Ireland during these times of horror, there is one from the then Supreme Pontiff, Innocent XII., dated at St. Mary Major, on the 10th of June, 1698. In this letter the holy father, after speaking in feeling language of the ordeal of persecution the church of Ireland had undergone, exhorts the prelates and people to confidence in the mercies of Him who suffered so much for the salvation of sinners. "Nor" (says he) "are your sufferings like those of yesterday; they are the sufferings of centuries; your nation, renowned for sanctity, has preserved for ages the glory of the faith, to your eternal honor, and the salvation of your souls. Therefore, suffer all things with Christian patience, knowing that the Lord will not permit any being to be tried beyond his strength.—As to us, our prayers shall be unceasing before the throne of mercy." Thus was Ireland situated in the reign of William. In the latter end of that reign, about the year 1698, the subject of this sketch was born, in the neighborhood of Mullingar, in the province of Leinster. His father belonged to that class commonly designated as "substantial country farmers," and finding in his son a desire to enter a college and prepare himself for the ministry, he determined to part with him, "it might be for years, it might be for ever," and procure him that education in a foreign college, which unjust laws deprived him of at home. Thus braving every danger, at a tender age the young aspirant embarked for France, and entered the college of Rheims, then celebrated for the learning and ability of its professors.

From the time of Mr. Mac-Geoghegan's entrance into this celebrated institution to the time of his ordination, I can find but very scanty means of information as regards his progress. This alone is certain, that he distinguished himself as a student of Philosophy, and obtained, in his general examination in Theology, the first prize afforded by the faculty at Rheims. Having obtained his sacerdotal ordination, he continued still in the College, acquiring further knowledge, and preaching occasionally in the churches of the city. About the year 1736, our historian went to England as chaplain to an English gentleman, whose name I have not been able to ascertain. During Mac-Geoghegan's engagement with this gentleman, he found means to travel into Ireland, and visit his native place. We may well imagine what were his feelings at the sight of the manifold sufferings and dreadful persecutions under which his poor countrymen were laboring. Having travelled through countries where his faith was triumphant, where respect was paid to conscientious conviction, where men were not "hanged and quartered" for worshipping God, where license was not given to a libertine soldiery to satiate their base appetites in defenceless villages, and there murder, in cold blood, large crowds of men, women, and children, he must have contemplated, in bitterness of heart, the melancholy scenes poor Ireland then presented. We next find Mr. Mac-Geoghegan in Paris, attached to one of its churches, actively engaged in the duties of the ministry. At this time his historical labors seem to have commenced: a time when exiled Irishmen displayed to the world their valor, their piety, and their prowess. In those days France numbered among her armies a corps, which none, even the most inveterate enemy of Ireland, dared deny to be the flower of chivalry, the saviours of France, the terror of England,—"The Irish Brigade." The illustrious "Dillon," foremost of the first, best of the good, bravest of the brave, witness to the broken treaty of Limerick, together with many others of his countrymen, went over to France, and there formed the gallant band of which he was unanimously appointed leader. In this place it is unnecessary to say any thing more about the "Irish Brigade." Their deeds of valor are matters of history: and the well-fought field of "Fontenoi," where,—at the soul-stirring watchword from the lips of Dillon, "Irishmen, remember Limerick!"—the tyrant Saxon persecutor bit the dust, or fled in confusion, before the thundering charge of the glorious exiles of poor Ireland, will be, while the world remains, the monument of their valor.

To this Brigade our historian had the honor of being chaplain. It was in very truth an enviable position. With what great and good men did it not give him perpetual intercourse! There was Dillon, Purcell, Cusack, Butler, and a host of others, in whose society Mac-Geoghegan spent much of his time. At the earnest request of many of the Irish exiles then in France, he compiled the present work in the French language, and dedicated it to the "Irish Brigade." As regards the merit of the work, one opinion has always prevailed, that among the many works already written on the subject, that by Mac-Geoghegan is unrivalled for discrimination, sound judgment, and freedom from all prejudice. Besides this, no writer could have within his reach better sources of testimony. The libraries of Paris, stored with the best works on Ireland, were perfectly at his disposal; and as to the important affairs connected with the reigns of James the First and Second, there could be no better means of acquiring information than those within the immediate reach of our writer. Mr. Mac-Geoghegan did not long enjoy the well-earned fame acquired by his literary labors. In the discharge of his holy duties a fever attacked him, and he died in the year 1750, regretted by his friends, (he had no enemies,) and was buried in Paris, where a simple slab records his name.

THE

HISTORY OF IRELAND,

ANCIENT AND MODERN.

HISTORY OF IRELAND.

PRELIMINARY DISCOURSE.

THE nation which forms the subject of this history is, without doubt, one of the most ancient in Europe.

An idea of its history must be agreeable to such as are desirous of exploring its antiquity. The situation of Ireland having rendered it difficult of access to invaders, her inhabitants lived during many ages free from all insult from their neighbors. They cultivated the arts, sciences, and letters, which they had borrowed from the most polished people of their time, the Egyptians and Phœnicians; and the patronage which their princes afforded to learning, joined to the esteem in which they held those who made a profession of it, contributed much to its advancement. A system of government founded on the laws of nature and humanity, influenced their morals. Some princes, possessed of a justice worthy of the first Christians, appeared like so many stars in an obscure night, from time to time upon the throne, and gave vigor to the laws enervated by the weakness of their predecessors.*

Ollam Fodla, one of their monarchs, summoned a triennial assembly at Teamor,† in order to regulate the affairs of the state, and to examine into the genealogies of families. He established schools for the cultivation of literature and philosophy, which the people had received from the ancients. Ugane-Mor, Aongus Tuirmeach, and Eocha Felioch, who had re-established the pentarchy, rendered jurisprudence vigorous, added new lustre to the laws, and granted a particular privilege to learning. Fearadach the Just, Feidlim the Legislator, Cormac Ulfada, and Cairbre the Second, surnamed Liffeachair, followed the example of their predecessors. The learned in jurisprudence who flourished in the different reigns, assisted the princes by their counsels.

Learning was not the sole occupation of the Scoto-Milesians; without mentioning their domestic wars, they often measured their arms, not only with the Picts, the Britons, and neighboring islanders, but with the Romans themselves, who were then the masters of the world. The expeditions of Eocha the Second, of Aongus Ollbuagach, son of Fiacha the First, Aongus the First, Ugane-Mor, Criomthan the First, Nial the Great, Dathy, and the dreadful devastations which they committed among the Britons, (of which Gildas complains,) furnish sufficient proofs of it.

The warlike character of the Scoto-Milesians appeared again, with splendor, in the long wars which they maintained against the Danes, and which lasted with doubtful success, from the beginning of the ninth century till 1014, when those barbarians were totally defeated at Clontarf by the valiant Brian Boroimhe, the monarch of the island; while they abandoned to them some other provinces, to free themselves of so formidable an enemy. Merit was not left unrewarded among them: the nobles were distinguished from each other, and they again from the people, by the number of colors, which each wore according to his rank. Enna the First ordered silver shields to be given to those chiefs who distinguished themselves in war; Muinemon added to them chains of gold, and Aldergode decreed gold rings as a reward to those who would distinguish themselves in the arts and sciences.

Lastly, the antiquaries, doctors, bards, or poets, called also "Fileas," were rewarded with lands, which had been assigned for them.

During the fifth century, Christianity presented new scenes in Ireland. That nation, so attached to the superstitions of paganism and idolatry, and versed in the theology of the Druids, became afterwards, by the preaching of the Gospel, the theatre of religion, and a seminary for strangers, while Gothic ignorance spread itself over the face of Europe. Thus, it may be said, that the four first ages of Christianity were the most brilliant, both of the ancient and modern history of that people; but the harmony of the

* Ante C. 720.

† Afterwards called Tara.

government and glory of Christianity became eclipsed in the ninth century, by the frequent invasions of the northern barbarians, who had overrun, about the same period, the greatest part of Europe. Their incursions continued for two centuries with doubtful success; the barbarians were often defeated, and in the end totally expelled.

The constitution of the state had been so shaken by this war, that it could never be re-established, notwithstanding the efforts which had been made. A decay in religion, and corruption in the morals of the people, from their intercourse with the barbarians; the interruption to the legitimate succession to the throne, which occurred about the time of Malachy the Second, by the intrusion of the provincial kings; and the different factions always attendant upon usurpation, brought insurmountable obstacles to its re-establishment, and were favorable circumstances to the ambition and cupidity of a neighboring nation.

Although history was cultivated among the Scoto-Milesians, more than among any of their contemporaries, notwithstanding also their great care to preserve to posterity the remembrance of their exploits; yet that people were but little known to the learned before Christianity. Strabo, Pomponius Mela, Solinus, and other writers, have made their ignorance appear, by giving arbitrary descriptions of this island, and by their exaggerated representations of the rudeness and barbarity of its inhabitants.

The English, having, in the twelfth century, put an end to the Irish monarchy, and wishing to give a color of justice to their usurpation, and to the tyranny which they exercised against the inhabitants of the country, have, without any other title than a fictitious bull of Adrian the Fourth, and the right of the strongest, represented the Irish as savages, who inhabited the woods,* and who never obeyed the laws, as if these titles were sufficient for stripping them of their properties.† What! that people so renowned in the first ages of Christianity for their piety and learning, and among whom the Anglo-Saxons themselves went, according to their own historians, to be instructed, during the centuries which preceded the invasion of the English, are all of a sudden reduced to the condition of savages!‡ The metamorphosis is too difficult to be admitted, and at the same time too obvious for us not to feel how absurd such an accusation must be. A nation that wishes to enslave others, generally treats those who will not submit to its laws as savages: a little attention, however, paid to the state in which Ireland then was, and to the pretensions of the English, will easily destroy the imposture. More than two thousand years had already elapsed, during which that people, commanded by native princes, were governed by their own laws; consequently they would not receive those of strangers, in whom they discovered neither character to inspire them with awe, nor power to make them obey. Although part of Ireland had at first submitted to the English, still more than two-thirds of it, far from bending under a yoke that seemed odious to them, were always under arms, to defend both their lives and properties against those tyrants. If he that repels an enemy, who comes armed to invade his patrimony, should be treated as a barbarian or a savage, the most polished nations and the most magnanimous merit the same appellations. Gerald Barry, a priest, and native of the country of Wales, in England, called in Latin, Cambria, (from whence is derived the name of Cambrensis, under which he is known,) was the first stranger who undertook to write the history of Ireland, in order to perpetuate the calumnies which his countrymen had already published against its inhabitants.

Circumstances required that they should make the Irish pass for barbarians. The title of Henry the Second was founded only upon a bull obtained clandestinely from Pope Adrian the Fourth, an Englishman by birth. The cause of this bull was a false statement which Henry had given to the Pope of the impiety and barbarism of the Irish nation. Cambrensis was then ordered to verify, by writing, the statement upon which the granting of the bull had been extorted. He did not fail to intermix his work with calumnies, and groundless absurdities; however, the credit of a powerful king knew how to make even the court of Rome believe them. It was in this spirit that Cambrensis wrote his history, and from thence the English authors have taken the false coloring under which ancient Ireland has been represented. Passion and interest made them pass over the recantation which Cambrensis felt himself obliged to make, in the latter part of his life, of several false and calumnious imputations, with which his history had been filled. Cambrensis did not possess the necessary requisites for an histo-

* Sylvestres Hiberni.

† Camd. edit. Lond. p. 730.

‡ "They retired hither, for the sake either of divine study, or a more chaste life."—*Bede's Church History*, b. 3, c. 27.